WINNING THE RECESSION

Small Business Action Guide to Remaining Profitable During a Recession

Version: January 17, 2023

Copyright © 2023 Don Kermath All Rights Reserved

www.DarkHorseSecrets.com
www.DonKermath.com

Dedication

To my partner Becca, who left breadcrumbs for me to find her after 35 years apart. I'm forever grateful for a second life that includes you. I'm also grateful for the forensic and honest review of this book. You helped me see what I am uniquely unqualified to see about my work.

To the experts and mentors who helped shape and mold me. I wish I had heeded more of your advice.

Introduction

The most successful businesses in the world are professionally run franchises. Sorry, the mom-and-pop stores are just not keeping up with the big brands. If you are going to survive and beat the big brands, you're going to have to start acting like a big brand but with a small brand charm.

Big brands understand how business systems, a collection of tested procedures, policies, and scripts, give them the advantage of scalability, teachability, and sustainability.

Dark Horse Mini Manifesto

My name is Don Kermath.

I'm part of a little-known group of small business owners you've probably never heard of.

We don't rely on venture capital or have delusions of going public. In fact, our smallness and diversity make up the charm and character of every town and city. We have products and services that we know enhance people's lives.

Because we're fighting against the big brands, corporations with literally unlimited budgets, we have to do things smarter. We don't have financial safety nets. Every dollar we risk is our own money. We have to be profitable from day one. So how do we do that? How is that even possible?

MBAs and college textbooks tell you what we are doing is impossible. Yet it's happening every day. It's happening through the art and science of Dark Horse Secrets.

We are Dark Horses.

We are just one system away.

Beat the big brands, and become a Dark Horse by joining our Facebook Group:

www.facebook.com/groups/darkhorsesecrets

Table of Contents

Dedication 3
Introduction 5
Table of Contents 7
Legal 9
    Disclaimer 9
    Copyright 9
How Recessions Affect Small Businesses 11
Cash Flow and Cash Reserves 15
Supply Chain Woes 19
Earn It or Pay for It Marketing 23
    Website and SEO 23
    Communication 24
    Social Media is Social 25
    Curb Appeal 26
Grants and Government Assistance 29
Raise Prices Increase Value 31
Add New Revenue Streams 33
    Create New Products and Services 34
    Take Inventory of Your Abilities 34
    Enter the International Market 35
    Offer Online Courses 35
    Develop Strategic Partnerships 36
    Sublet Your Office Space 37
    Follow the Market Trends 37
    Seize Potential Opportunities 38
In God We Trust, Everyone Else Bring Data 41
Hedgehog Concept 43
Invest in Your Existing Customers 45

Winning Cost Savings Opportunities ... 47
Reduce Payroll Expenses ... 47
Automate and Systematize ... 48
Inventory Management ... 49
Negotiate Your Rent ... 50
Shop Your Utilities ... 50
Shop Your Credit Card Processor ... 50
Shop All Your Suppliers ... 50
Cancel Ineffective Advertising ... 51
Reduce Your Tax Burden - Legally ... 51
Save on Office and Cleaning Supplies ... 51
Install Smart Thermostats ... 51
Cancel or Reduce Subscriptions ... 52
Buy Used ... 52
Credit Card Reward Programs ... 53

Continue Staff & Guest Wellness Procedures ... 55
Winning the Recession Action List ... 59
Final Words ... 61
References ... 63
Ask for Help ... 65
About the Author ... 67
Hire Superstar Part-Time Employees ... 67
Can I Ask a Favor? ... 68

Legal

Disclaimer

I'm not an attorney, accountant, or plumber—do not construe any advice here to be legal, financial, or plumbing in nature. My successes and failures are my own. You might succeed or fail epically. **Hopefully, you'll learn from my failures to avoid your own**, but that is out of my control. You are the chef in your kitchen.

Although the author and publisher have made every effort to ensure that the information in this document was correct at press time, the author and publisher do not assume and hereby disclaim any liability to any party for any loss, damage, or disruption caused by errors or omissions, whether such errors or omissions result from negligence, accident, or any other cause.

Copyright

Copyright © 2023 Don Kermath All Rights Reserved.
Cover design with Canva.com by Don Kermath

How Recessions Affect Small Businesses

"I am ready to face any challenges that might be foolish enough to face me." — Dwight, The Office TV Show

A recession is defined as an economic downturn where there are two consecutive negative-growth quarters. Frequently the economy experiences higher unemployment, reduced manufacturing, and consumers spend less.

This recession is primarily caused by the government's reaction to the Coronavirus pandemic. The lockdowns caused immediate damage to the economy and the subsequent "free" money caused artificial excess demand. That demand and worker's slow return to work caused supply chain issues. The supply chain issues, both product and labor, contributed to high inflation.

Now the consensus is that we are entering a recession. However, this is not the same as recent recessions according to Dr. David Phelps (Phelps, 2022).

> *"We've had 40 years, from 1980 to 2020, where we've had disinflation and low-interest rates, but then we turn the corner to face completely new rules. We have rapidly growing inflation now, and as a result, higher interest rates. This means we have to learn how to do things differently." Dr. David Phelps, Inflation: The Silent Retirement Killer*

This all means that to win during this recession you must adopt new strategies. If not, the cost of doing business will eat into your profit margin.

The U.S. Chamber of Commerce 3rd Quarter 2022 Small Business Index (US Chamber of Commerce, 2022) survey claims 88% of business owners are concerned about the U.S. entering an economic downturn in the next year. The U.S. Chamber of Commerce 4th Quarter 2022 Small Business Index (US Chamber of Commerce, 2022) reports only 27% of small business owners believe the U.S. economy is in good health, a slight decrease over Q3 2022. Additionally, the Consumer Price Index rose 7.1% for the 12 months ending in November 2022.

To make matters worse, small businesses are frequently hit hardest by a recession and inflation due to a lack of readiness.

The good news is small business owners appear to be somewhat optimistic about the future. The U.S. Chamber of Commerce Small Business Index climbed after the start of the COVID-19 pandemic, but not yet to pre-pandemic levels. The bad news is that the Index dipped in Q3 2022 and remained there for Q4 2022 due to persistently high inflation.

Small Business Index Q4 2019 – Q4 2022 (US Chamber of Commerce, 2022)

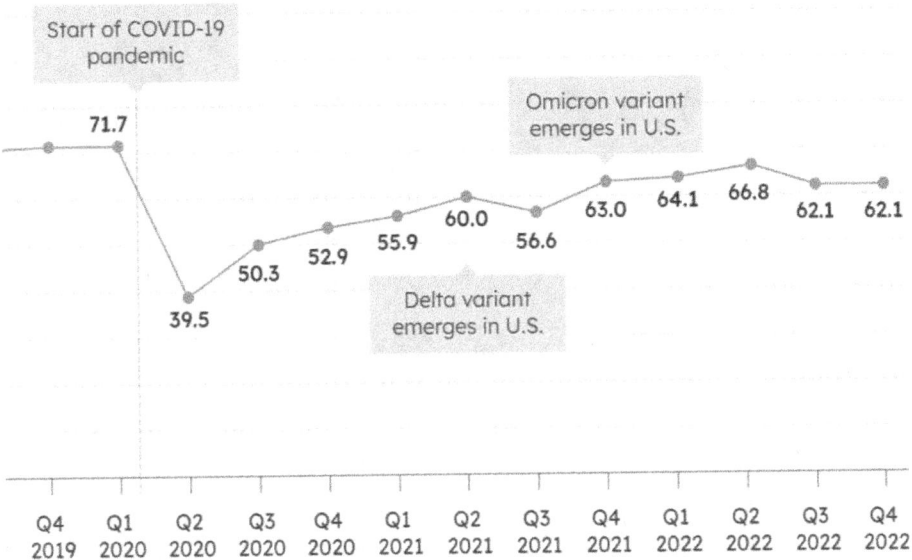

A few businesses will thrive during a recession and increase profits while most will see profits decline. If you want to win the recession, however, you must take actionable steps now.

This Action Guide is designed to help you win the recession and remain profitable. There is no reason your business can't win the recession – here's how to take advantage of opportunities during a recession.

Cash Flow and Cash Reserves

"We were always focused on our profit and loss statement. But cash flow was not a regularly discussed topic. It was as if we were driving along, watching only the speedometer, when in fact we were running out of gas." — Michael Dell, founder and CEO, Dell Technologies

Cash flow can be the biggest issue concerning small businesses. Without sufficient cash reserves, you must rely on prompt accounts receivables to meet operating expenses. During a recession, your clients might be slow to pay or may not be able to pay you at all.

How do you know if you have sufficient cash reserves? The general rule is to always have three to six months of cash to cover operating expenses. That might be too much or too little for your situation. If you answer yes to the following questions consider leaning towards six months instead of three.

1. Is your business seasonal? If it is your off-season now, you will struggle longer until your season comes around.
2. Are you reluctant or unable to access short-term financing? Short-term financing could get you through a tough spell. Remember, servicing that debt becomes a

fixed expense for the business. Higher interest rates might make financing untenable. Borrowing money to meet cash flow problems during a prolonged recession could be problematic for any future recovery.

3. Are your fixed expenses greater than your variable expenses? As your revenue decreases, your fixed expenses become a greater percentage of your revenue. You'll need more cash reserves to meet these expenses during a recession.

There are three important cash flow formulas to know about:

- ✓ Free Cash Flow = Net income + Depreciation/Amortization – Change in Working Capital – Capital Expenditure
- ✓ Operating Cash Flow = Operating Income + Depreciation – Taxes + Change in Working Capital
- ✓ Cash Flow Forecast = Beginning Cash + Projected Inflows – Projected Outflows = Ending Cash

To learn more about these formulas use the following search string in your favorite online search engine:

> 🔍 How to calculate cash flow

Here are a couple of websites I found useful:
www.waveapps.com/blog/cash-flow-formula

blog.embarkwithus.com/cash-flow-worksheet-template-basics-best-practices

Winning Pro Tip:

Make accounts receivable a priority. Consider offering incentives for prompt payment. Many businesses build the incentive into the initial price. That way, instead of just a late-payment penalty as the stick, your clients get a reward as the carrot for prompt payment. Your net is the same.

For example, a landlord needs to get $1,000/mo for a rental unit. Set the monthly rate at $1,100 with a $100 deduction for prompt payment. There can still be a late payment penalty, but the opportunity to save $100 every month is highly motivating for the tenant.

Supply Chain Woes

"The amateurs discuss tactics: the professionals discuss logistics." — Napoleon Bonaparte

For decades, small businesses had few supply chain concerns. This recession has changed the rules.

Logically your supplier should be happy for your business during a recession. It seems like so many suppliers are ill-prepared to meet the demands.

Your goal is to make sure you have everything you need to run your business at the most affordable price possible.

Identify key inputs – the things and services required to make your product or provide your service. During the pandemic of 2020, even toilet paper became scarce. Don't forget to include services in your input needs. Equipment has to be maintained.

Here are some key questions to ask about your input needs:

1. Is the input already hard to find? Disposable latex or nitrile gloves were impossible to get during the 2020 pandemic. Now is the time to locate multiple sources and stock up.
2. Does it take a long time to get the input? Currently, it could take several months to get a pickup truck. Now is the time to look forward to your expected needs. Place

your orders now, especially if the order can be canceled without penalty.

3. Is the input expensive? A delivery vehicle is expensive, for example. Now is the time to figure out financing for expensive inputs. Will you require a loan? Can you service the new debt? How much can you set aside now for this future expense?

4. Is the price likely to go up significantly? Cooking oil has seen significant increases in just 12 months. It is hard to predict pricing, but inflation is going to cause everything to go up. Can you afford to stock up now, so you won't have to pay a premium during the recession? Of course, this works best with things that don't expire.

5. Will a lack of this input shut down your operation? Labor is an example of this kind of input. If you are not doing so, now is the time to look for superstars. Your job number one is to constantly hire superstars and set free those whose talents and disposition are best suited somewhere else.

If the answer is yes to any of these questions, now is the time to figure out how you would acquire those inputs and make a plan.

To learn more use the following search string in your favorite online search engine:

🔍 supply chain management for small business

Here are a couple of websites I found useful:
sbdctampabay.com/6-best-practices-in-supply-chain-management/
www.forbes.com/sites/theyec/2021/12/07/six-ways-small-businesses-can-overcome-supply-chain-challenges/

Winning Pro Tip:

Identify suppliers who have coop and spiff programs. Many manufacturers will pay you when you sell more of their products. You might even be able to set up exclusivity agreements that ensure you get supplied before anyone else.

Coop programs generally involve getting reimbursed for advertising. If you follow the manufacturer's instructions, you can get a percentage of your wholesale costs back in a rebate check. Spiff programs generally pay you a rebate check based on units sold.

Earn It or Pay for It Marketing

"I market for the same reason a pilot keeps his engines running once he is off the ground." — William Wrigley, Jr.

Big businesses can afford to buy all the marketing they need. Small businesses, even in the best of times, struggle to find resources to buy marketing. The good news is that you can earn marketing that costs you time but little money.

Website and SEO

Your company website and good search engine optimization (SEO) are often responsible for the first contact with your customer. Make sure your website is mobile responsive or at least mobile friendly. Search engines favor websites with mobile responsiveness.

Visit your competitors' websites. How do you compare? When you search for your product or service where does your business show up on the search engine hierarchy? The higher you are the better your SEO.

Have you ever heard the joke about where is the best place to hide a dead body? Answer: on page 2 of the search engine results.

Search online for ways to improve your website's SEO. You should be able to make the necessary fixes to your website on your own if you have control of your website design tools. Improving SEO takes time and continuous effort. Stick with it and you'll reap the rewards.

To learn more use the following search string in your favorite online search engine:

> 🔍 diy seo

Communication

There is no way to understate the importance of keeping in touch with your staff and customers during tough times. You don't want your customers to forget about you. You've spent years and countless dollars getting top-of-mind awareness with them. Don't let that all go to waste during a recession.

1. Ideally, you have an email and text database for your customers. Continue to reach out once a week to let them know what you are doing to be ready for them when they are ready to buy again.
2. Stay in touch with the staff you had to set free due to reduced revenue but wish to rehire when things change for the better. Give them honest assessments of the situation. Let them know what you are doing to bring them back to work as quickly as possible.

3. Communicate any new offerings, policies, and procedures you plan to implement.
4. Share your personal story. What are you doing to keep your spirits up and how you are excited to get back to serving your customers?

To learn more use the following search strings in your favorite online search engine:

> 🔍 email best practices for small business
> 🔍 sms best practices for small business

Social Media is Social

Social media comes in many forms - Facebook, Instagram, Twitter, and TikTok to name a few. Each has its unique demographics. It is better to pick one and do it well than to work multiple mediums poorly.

This is a great way to remain social with your customers, even if they've stopped frequenting your business during the recession. They'll remember you when times get better. Just remember it's called social media for a reason – be social. Your customers don't want to be sold 24/7. Nine of out ten posts should be informational or entertaining. The tenth post can be about your offerings.

To learn more use the following search string in your favorite online search engine:

> 🔍 social media best practices for small business

Curb Appeal

Have you ever heard about how important curb appeal is when selling a home? Well, the same is true for your retail location.

Are your doors and windows clean? Is the parking lot policed and tidy? Are all the exterior lights and signs working properly?

HGTV has an online list of things to improve curb appeal under $100 for your home that could work for your small business as well.

1. Paint the front door.
2. Plant a tree or two.
3. Install plant boxes or flowerpots.
4. Clean and pressure wash.
5. Coordinate colors.
6. Display your address or suite number with style.
7. Update exterior lighting.
8. Make an inviting seating area.
9. Use big rocks to fill voids. They can double as seating.
10. Define your entry. It should not be difficult to find the entrance to your business.
11. Manicure any lawn and landscaping.

By the way, your website has a form of curb appeal too. Is it messy, or hard to read? Are the colors coordinated? Make sure your website has curb appeal too.

To learn more use the following search string in your favorite online search engine:

> 🔍 diy retail curb appeal

Winning Pro Tip:

Your street signage is the single most important form of customer communication. The better your business location and consequently the visual intrusiveness of your street sign the less you have to spend on advertising elsewhere.

1. Make sure the sign is in good working order.
2. If the sign is old and faded, consider replacing it.
3. The sign should be located where it is most intrusively visible.
4. Buy the largest sign your local building codes and lease terms allow.

Grants and Government Assistance

"Man becomes great exactly in the degree in which he works for the welfare of his fellow men."
— Mahatma Gandhi

As a small business, you pay taxes on just about everything. Depending on your state, county, and city you are probably paying income, property, sales, use, unemployment, medicare, social security, and worker's compensation taxes. Yes, some of these are called insurance, but if the government is forcing you to buy it is a tax.

You should not feel bad about getting some of that tax money back in the form of grants and government assistance. Search online for grants and government programs for small businesses. Just be careful not to fall prey to scammers assisting you with getting those grants or assistance.

To learn more use the following search strings in your favorite online search engine:

🔍 small business grants
🔍 small business grants for women
🔍 small business grants for minorities
🔍 small business grants for veterans

> 🔍 small business grants [enter your city name here]
> 🔍 small business grants [enter your state name here]
> 🔍 small business grants [enter your business sector here]

Helpful websites:

www.sba.gov/funding-programs/grants

www.grants.gov/learn-grants/grant-making-agencies/small-business-administration.html

Winning Pro Tip:

There are hundreds if not thousands of private grant programs for small businesses. Expand your online search to include large private corporations. LegalZoom.com has a grant program, for example.

Raise Prices Increase Value

"Price is what you pay. Value is what you get." — *Warren Buffett*

Many small businesses are reluctant to raise prices for fear they will lose customers. The reality is that you cannot stay in business to service those customers if you are not profitable. Now is the time to raise prices as your customers expect prices to go up during high inflationary times.

First, price increases should be part of your normal business strategy. Dramatic onerous price increases could send customers elsewhere. If you raise prices, on some things, twice a year and in small increments, you'll find it easier for your customers to absorb the increases.

Second, evaluate your offerings for value. How can you increase prices while simultaneously adding value to your offerings? Many retailers offer "free gifts with purchase" as a way to increase value, for example. Of course, the cost of the free gift cannot be greater than the price increase.

If you provide a service, how can you not only add value but differentiate yourself from your competition? Being the cheapest, like Wal-Mart, can be a winning marketing strategy, but being the second cheapest is a losing strategy. Having the greatest value and highest price is the most profitable strategy. Don't be afraid to raise prices while increasing value.

To learn more use the following search string in your favorite online search engine:

> 🔍 small business pricing strategy

Winning Pro Tip:

A winning pricing strategy exemplifies value, confidence, and influence. A low, cheap price, might mean the product or service is poorly made or won't work. A higher price conveys a higher value and confidence in your product or service. However, if your price is too low or too high your product or service might be overlooked. The right price will influence a positive buying decision.

Keep testing the price ceiling. Figure out at what point net revenues peak. Note I said net revenue. Sometimes an increase in gross revenue can translate into a decrease in net revenue. Also, recognize the difference between a percentage increase/decrease and a real dollar increase/decrease. As my banker once told me, you can't put a percentage in the bank.

Add New Revenue Streams

"Business is all about solving people's problems — at a profit." — Paul Marsden

Adding new revenue streams is easier said than done. The risk is getting involved in something that takes away attention from your core business. That being said, find new revenue closely related to your core business that serves your same customers. A tanning salon could offer spa services. A flower shop could add gift baskets. A bakery could add specialty coffee. Your customers are going to buy these things somewhere, why shouldn't they buy them from you?

Here are eight small business new revenue stream tips from the Service Corps of Retired Executives (SCORE) (Farmiloe, 2021):

Create New Products and Services

"The best way to create a new revenue stream is to develop additional new products and services when possible. Be innovative and look to offer a product or service you've never offered before. This year, we expanded our product line to include TV screen protectors, something that was new to us that we saw the opportunity." — Peter Babichenko, SaharaCase

Take Inventory of Your Abilities

"When creating a new revenue stream, it is crucial to take inventory of your abilities and processes. Your new revenue stream should be closely aligned with your main offering that doesn't subtract from your limited resources to ensure profitability. The key is to challenge how you look at various forms of waste and determine how to turn it into money!" — Noah Downs, American Pipeline Solutions

Enter the International Market

"Our business has been selling fashion-branded watches like Emporio Armani, Tissot, and Garmin since 2007. We decided to open up an online retail watch store in the US to develop our brand on an international scale. Sometimes, entering a new market can not only open up new revenue streams, but the expansion can also open up new ways of doing business." — Daniel Richmond, Tic Watches

Offer Online Courses

"It's no great surprise that many small businesses are struggling. Even as we begin to approach more normalcy, there is still revenue loss to attempt to regain. One specific avenue that can help bring in additional revenue is to offer online courses on topics where you will be considered an expert. It is less complicated than one might think, especially when you have knowledge that can be shared with other companies or individuals that can also help them regain lost revenue." — Greg Kozera, ELM Learning

Develop Strategic Partnerships

"Sometimes, developing new revenue streams doesn't require new products or services. It just requires a new approach to connecting your products or services to customers. Partner with like-minded brands or complementary service providers to open up referrals. For our business, partnering with brands like Mailchimp, GoDaddy, and even SCORE has helped us connect with the small business owners we enjoy working with. And for our partners, there's a mutual delivery of value that makes the partnership worthwhile. Think about how you can create value for a partner first and then make a pitch." — Brett Farmiloe, Markitors

Sublet Your Office Space

"With so many small businesses taking a hit with all of the COVID shutdowns getting creative with new revenue streams is a must. Many restaurants adopted delivery and meal preparation services to offset the lack of patrons visiting their businesses. Other types of companies would sublet their space to keep themselves in business during their slowdowns. It all comes down to repurposing your resources so you can still earn revenue to stay open. Getting creative with what you have and what you can offer is essential to staying afloat during tough times." — Mark Smith, UAT

Follow the Market Trends

"Sometimes there are revenue opportunities from new consumer trends. For example, in the pandemic, there was a huge increase in boat and RV sales. For our business that meant offering and marketing products like our boat insurance policies. By following market trends, a business can adjust its marketing efforts and product line to meet consumer demand." — Brandon Berglund, Berglund Insurance

Seize Potential Opportunities

"Small businesses need to diversify their product offering to ensure they aren't putting all their eggs in one basket. As a Historic Hotel & Restaurant located in the picturesque North Georgia Mountains, we started hosting small weddings on the property. We realized this was a huge opportunity we were not taking full advantage of. Since then, we have built our wedding business and opened a new, larger wedding venue called Forest Lodge. We are excited to welcome even more brides and a new revenue stream for our company." — Gwen North, Lake Rabun Hotel

To learn more use the following search strings in your favorite online search engine:

> 🔍 how to create new revenue streams
> 🔍 how to create additional revenue streams
> 🔍 how to create new income streams

Winning Pro Tip:

An ideal revenue stream does not require you to work more hours in the week. The idea is to find additional revenue streams that fall within your core business concept and allow you to enjoy life at the same time. Use those two criteria to reject or accept new revenue stream ideas in their infancy.

In God We Trust, Everyone Else Bring Data

"It is a capital mistake to theorize before one has data." — Sherlock Holmes

Small businesses have the advantage of quick reaction times. This is only valuable if you are looking at key metrics daily. Here are some key short-term metrics:

1. Gross revenue: Constantly compare to the same day, week, month, and quarter from the previous year. Identify the cause of any drastic changes. Is it due to the economy or is it due to a training issue? If you catch the issue quickly you can make the necessary changes.
2. Gross expense: Controlling your expense is the single most important path to profitability. Keep close track of your expenses.
3. Net revenue: Gross revenue and gross expense tell one story. Net revenue tells you if your efforts to fix revenue or expense issues are paying off. If you increase gross

revenue but your variable expenses increase more than the revenue your net will be down.
4. Revenue per customer: This metric can tell you whether your new revenue streams are working. When the number of customers is declining your best option is to increase the revenue per customer.
5. Employee sales: You hire employees for one purpose – to make a profit for the business owners. Continuously monitor revenue per employee. Consider replacing or retraining any employee not generating enough profit for the business owners.

To learn more use the following search string in your favorite online search engine:

🔍 key metrics for small business

Winning Pro Tip:

Another key metric to monitor is your customers' financial health. Are your customers becoming slower to pay or even not paying at all? It might be time to reduce or change credit terms for some of your customers to avoid cash flow issues later.

Hedgehog Concept

"The fox has many tricks. The hedgehog has but one. But that is the best of all." — Ralph Waldo Emerson

The hedgehog concept, as stated in Jim Collin's book *Good to Great*, is,

"A simple, crystalline concept that flows from deep understanding about the intersection of three circles: 1) what you are deeply passionate about, 2) what you can be the best in the world at, and 3) what best drives your economic or resource engine. Transformations from good to great come about by a series of good decisions made consistently with a Hedgehog Concept, supremely well executed, accumulating one upon another, over a long period of time."

The intersection of these three circles is also known as your core product or service. Refocusing on your core business and eliminating side hustles that divert your attention is a winning strategy during a recession.

The hedgehog concept can also be called a unique selling proposition. What is your hedgehog concept? Define it. Focus on it. Eliminate everything else that does not support your core business. You will make more money with this laser focus than being scattered across many unrelated business concepts. Think about Midas Muffler, Kentucky Fried Chicken, Chik-fil-A, and Duncan Donuts. Do one thing and do it well.

To learn more use the following search string in your favorite online search engine:

> 🔍 unique selling proposition for small business

Winning Pro Tip:

An exercise we like to perform is called, "What would we do if we had to compete with ourselves?" Often the answer to this question is your next business opportunity. The answer to this question will also reveal weaknesses in any perceived competitive advantage you thought you had.

Invest in Your Existing Customers

"The strength of brand loyalty begins with how your product makes people feel." — Jay Samit

Acquiring new customers is exciting, but maintaining existing ones is cheaper and they tend to spend more money. Since resources get tighter during a recession, it gets even harder to bring in new business.

Let your existing customers know you value their patronage and loyalty. Start or enhance a loyalty rewards program. This can be as simple as a punch card and as complicated as an online portal. Don't forget to consider starting a membership option for your product or service. Memberships are a form of a loyalty reward program.

To learn more use the following search strings in your favorite online search engine:

> 🔍 loyalty rewards programs for small business
> 🔍 how to retain customers for small business

Winning Pro Tip:

How you handle customer complaints goes a long way to retaining existing customers.

Here is our recipe for correcting our screw-ups:

Listen with empathy (take notes). I'm constantly amazed at how many upset guests calm down and feel relieved just to have someone listen to them. They only need to vent—they ask for nothing.

Repeat the issue back to the guest as you now understand it (this shows you are empathetic and demonstrates that you understand the real issue).

Apologize and explain that it won't happen again (make sure it doesn't happen again through policy and training if necessary).

Ask the guest what you can do to fix the issue (do not assume you know what the guest wants).

If it is reasonable, and it usually is, implement the fix. If it is unreasonable, offer a reasonable solution. You don't want to go bankrupt, but you also don't want a bad online review. (We are often able to give the guest an entire refund for a service or product they used but were unsatisfied with, for example, if they are willing to take the refund in the form of store credit.)

Many managers and business owners dread dealing with a complaint or unsatisfied customer. **I look forward to the opportunity to right a wrong—win back a customer lost**. Statistically, 80% of your clients will continue to do business with you if you properly and quickly handle your screw-up. I like those odds.

Winning Cost Savings Opportunities

"It's not how much money you make, but how much money you keep, how hard it works for you, and how many generations you keep it for." — *Robert Kiyosaki*

You might be scrambling to figure out ways to make money during a recession, but have you considered ways to save money? Why is this more important than figuring out ways to make more money? Think about it; every dollar you make may only result in 15 cents of profit at the bottom of your financial statement. But every dollar you save goes directly to the bottom line. **It is ALL profit.**

Ah, now you get it. Sort your profit and loss statement from last year with the largest expenses on top and the smallest on the bottom. The top is where the biggest gains are made - start there.

Here are some ways to save money:

Reduce Payroll Expenses

Ask yourself some poignant questions.

Is there anyone on my staff I would not hire if they came looking for a job today? If yes, now is the time to clean your house.

Can we reduce our hours without compromising service? Every hour reduced saves hundreds or even thousands of dollars annually. If you have multiple locations, can you consolidate them into fewer locations?

Are there any positions that can be combined or eliminated? Do you contract for services, like janitorial, bookkeeping, and landscaping? Can any of those services be moved in-house without increasing the net cost? Can you reduce the frequency of those services?

Automate and Systematize

The most successful businesses in the world are professionally run franchises. Sorry, the mom-and-pop stores are just not keeping up with the big brands. If you are going to survive and beat the big brands, especially during a recession, you're going to have to start acting like a big brand but with a small brand charm.

Big brands understand how business systems, a collection of tested procedures, policies, and scripts, give them the advantage of scalability, teachability, and sustainability.

Your small businesses' smallness and diversity make up the charm and character of your town. You have products and services that you know enhance people's lives.

Because you're fighting against the big brands, corporations with literally unlimited budgets, you have to do things smarter. You don't have financial safety nets. Every dollar you risk is your money. You have to be profitable from day one. So how do you do that? How is that even possible?

MBAs and college textbooks tell you what you are doing is impossible. Yet it's happening every day. It's happening through the art and science of business systems. It's time to play like the big brands and automate and systematize your operations.

Here is a thought exercise to help you get started automating and systematizing. Imagine you could not step foot into your business for three months, one full quarter. What would you do to prepare your business for your absence? The answer to that question will be a series of automated and manual procedures, policies, and scripts so anyone could run your business.

You don't have to get your entire business automated and systematized all at once. Start with the tasks that consume most of your time. Once you have this time-suck off of your plate you'll have more time to automate and systematize more aspects of your business. If you're going to win the recession and compete with the big brands, you'll want to automate and systematize now.

Inventory Management

Even if you don't sell a product you have an inventory – office and cleaning supplies, coffee and tea, equipment, parts, and even staff make up your inventory.

Evaluate all your inventory and locate inventory you can reduce or eliminate. Don't forget to look at the staff. Can anything be reduced without sacrificing service or product quality or reliability? Sometimes this might mean ordering more so you can realize a better price. Often, just changing the supplier can have a significant impact on the cost of your inventory. Remember, every dollar saved goes straight to the bottom line – profit.

Negotiate Your Rent

Commercial real estate is going to see a significant increase in vacancies these coming months and next year. Hire a consultant if you don't feel competent or know where to begin.

Shop Your Utilities

You might not know this, but in most areas, you can choose a different energy provider. Search online for energy providers in your area and make them bid on your business' energy needs.

Shop Your Credit Card Processor

If you accept credit cards shop around for another credit card processing company. A one percent savings in fees will save $1,000 per year on every $100,000 in credit card sales.

Shop All Your Suppliers

You've built a long-term relationship with many of your suppliers. Some of them feel more like family than business associates. Don't let that emotional bond interfere with the livelihood of your business and your employees. Audit your supplier agreements. Are they competitive? Where do you buy your inventory? Is there a supplier who can meet your needs and provide better pricing and service? Sometimes you don't have to switch, you just need to present your current supplier with a proposal from a new supplier.

Cancel Ineffective Advertising

If you don't know if your advertising is working you might consider canceling it or at least refocusing those resources on advertising campaigns you know are working.

Reduce Your Tax Burden - Legally

Many small businesses miss legitimate business expenses, like a business cellphone, home office, and business use of a personal vehicle. Stop using your personal cash and credit cards for business expenses. Dedicate separate accounts and credit cards for business use. Consult your tax accountant for opportunities to save money on taxes.

Save on Office and Cleaning Supplies

If you are using a janitor and office supply house that delivers your supplies, you are probably overpaying. Get a club membership, like Sam's Club, or order online to save a bundle on supplies and have them delivered to your doorstep. Consider technology that will make your business paperless or more paperless. You'll save on paper and printer ink.

Install Smart Thermostats

Properly installed and configured smart thermostats can pay for themselves in a month or two. After that, it's all money in the bank from utility savings. Smart thermostats can recognize usage patterns and automatically maximize your utility usage for optimum savings.

Cancel or Reduce Subscriptions

Netflix, Hulu, mobile carriers, cable TV, Point of Sale software, Spotify, and QuickBooks are just a few of the numerous subscription services a small business acquires over time. First, identify everything that is automatically billed to your business checking and credit card accounts. Next, cancel services you don't need to run your business. As well, many providers will lower your rate just by giving them a call with a desire to switch to another provider or to cancel. Finally, see if there is a reduced version of the service. Many businesses have bundled deals with cable providers, but don't need everything in the bundle. See if your service will be cheaper unbundled and with reduced services.

Wave accounting software is free and just as versatile as QuickBooks. Wave provides full-service payroll options that are competitive with QuickBooks.

Buy Used

Buying equipment one to three years used is a great way to get the latest technology without paying a premium. Buying used means you save the steep depreciation that often happens during the first few years. Some of your competitors who have purchased new equipment will not survive the recession. Look out for opportunities to buy gently used equipment at a reduced price.

Credit Card Reward Programs

You use credit card reward programs for your personal finances, why don't you use them for your small business? Many banks offer rewards programs on debit cards too. There is no excuse for using credit or debit cards without rewards associated with them. You are giving away money; in some cases, it can be 5% or even 11% cash back on all purchases.

CAUTION: If you do not pay off your credit debt monthly then the best credit cards are the ones with the lowest interest rate. Otherwise, you'll easily eat up any rewards and then some in high credit card interest. By the way, paying down that high-interest debt first is a winning financial strategy.

To learn more use the following search string in your favorite online search engine:

> 🔍 cost saving strategies for small business

Winning Pro Tip:

If you are the kind of person who is afraid to negotiate, remember this one piece of advice. The worst thing anyone can say in a negotiation is, "No."

Continue Staff & Guest Wellness Procedures

"It is health that is real wealth and not pieces of gold and silver." — *Mahatma Gandhi*

Your staff and guests have fears and concerns that didn't exist just months ago. How you deal with these fears and concerns will determine if they continue to frequent your business. Additionally, State and Federal agencies may require wellness procedures as a condition for staying open for business.

Here is a suggested list of wellness procedures. Pick and choose which ones work best for your business and the threat assessment level.

1. Upgrade your cleaning and sanitation procedures post-pandemic. Increase the frequency of cleaning and sanitizing public spaces such as the door handles, front desk, bathrooms, elevators, stairwells, and meeting areas.

2. Develop and implement workforce contact tracing following an employee pathogen-positive test. Informing staff and guests of contact with a contagious person is one way to contain a pathogen's spread.

3. Implement a face-covering policy that makes staff and guests feel most comfortable.
4. Install touchless hand-sanitizer stations just inside your front door - this will make guests feel safe coming into and leaving your business.
5. Identify how to maintain social distancing among staff and guests.
    a. Move cash drawers six feet apart.
    b. Place floor decals encouraging social distancing.
    c. Implement online staff training.
6. Develop employee hygiene guidelines.
    a. Stay home or work from home if you have a cough or low-grade fever of 99.1°F/37.3°C or more. Contact and follow the advice of your medical provider. Isolating yourself prevents the spread of pathogens.
    b. Wash hands with soap and water frequently. Washing kills most pathogens.
    c. Avoid touching your face. Face coverings help with this. Contact transfer from hands to mouth, nose, ears, or eyes is one-way to infect yourself with a pathogen.
    d. Sneeze or cough into a tissue or inside of your elbow. This reduces the spread of pathogens.
    e. Disinfect frequently used items and surfaces like telephones, mobile devices, keyboards, mice, and

counters. Surface contamination is one-way pathogens can spread.

    f. Use face coverings when inside buildings and in the presence of other people. This reduces the spread of pathogens.

7. Market these new and improved procedures to your staff and guests. This will make everyone feel safe and secure working in and visiting your business.

To learn more use the following search string in your favorite online search engine:

> 🔍 wellness advice for small business

Winning Pro Tip:

Even business owners, maybe especially business owners, need to take a mental health day off.

Winning the Recession Action List

"Complexity is the enemy of execution" – Tony Robbins

- ☑ Brace yourself for a protracted recession and recovery
- ☑ Get a handle on your cash flow needs
- ☑ Build your cash reserves – it's never too late to start
- ☑ Build redundancies in your supply chain
- ☑ Fine-tune your marketing efforts
- ☑ Seek assistance from grant programs
- ☑ Raise prices while increasing the value
- ☑ Add new revenue streams without sacrificing your core business
- ☑ Identify key metrics and check them at least weekly
- ☑ Clarify your unique selling proposition
- ☑ Invest in your existing customers – there's a goldmine here
- ☑ Locate smart cost savings without sacrificing customer service
- ☑ Maintain your health - trading health for wealth is a losing strategy
- ☑ Ask for help – you don't have to do it all alone

Final Words

"When you are grateful, fear disappears and abundance appears." — Tony Robbins

Don't just survive the recession, plan on winning the recession. Being small has the advantage of reduced overhead, nimble agility, and quick decision-making. Use some or all of these winning strategies to come out of this recession stronger and more profitable than ever.

References

Farmiloe, B. (2021, March 25). *8 Ways To Develop & Create New Revenue Streams In a Small Business.* Retrieved from SCORE: https://www.score.org/blog/8-ways-develop-create-new-revenue-streams-small-business

Phelps, D. D. (2022). *Inflation: The Silent Retirement Killer.* Dpi Media, LLC.

US Chamber of Commerce. (2022). *Small Business Index Q3 2022: The Voice of Small Business Owners.* US Chamber of Commerce.

US Chamber of Commerce. (2022). *Small Business Index Q4 2022: The Voice of Small Business Owners.* US Chamber of Commerce.

Ask for Help

"Ask for help. Not because you are weak. But because you want to remain strong." — Les Brown

It's one thing to have a plan, it's another to implement it. If this all seems overwhelming. If you just don't know where to begin. If you're not sure you can execute effectively. If you're feeling like you're all alone. **Ask for help.**

Your small business recovery is a multi-faceted problem. It's not as simple as "making a plan" or "throwing money at the problem." It's much more about execution, no matter the challenge. When you are held accountable, you succeed. **Yes, you CAN** successfully overcome the challenges of winning the recession, if you can execute your plan.

Don Kermath is the small business recovery expert that has been empowering small business leaders to transform their businesses into profit centers again. If that sounds like a miracle task, you need Don's influence in your small business more than ever. **He'll help you go from desperation and despair to growth and profit.** All of this is possible while you improve your ability to remain profitable in the face of a recession, pandemic, or any dire situation.

You can reach Don at his website: www.donkermath.com

About the Author

Don Kermath is an Amazon #1 best-selling author and is the employee turnover reduction expert that empowers small business owners and managers to transform their workforce into productive, cohesive, team-players who stay for the long haul and contribute to innovation and excellence on the job (and could really benefit your bottom line).

You can reach Don at his website: www.donkermath.com

Hire Superstar Part-Time Employees

Get your copy today of the Amazon #1 New Release and discover little-known ways small businesses can find, employ, and keep more qualified, competent, and motivated people.
amzn.to/3dK4Cbc

Can I Ask a Favor?

If you enjoyed this book, found it useful, or otherwise then I'd really appreciate it if you would post a short review on Amazon. I especially would love to hear what you loved about the book. I read all the reviews personally so that I can continually write what people are wanting.

If you'd like to leave a review then please visit the book page and leave a review: **www.amazon.com/dp/B0BS73SBGW**

Thanks for your support!

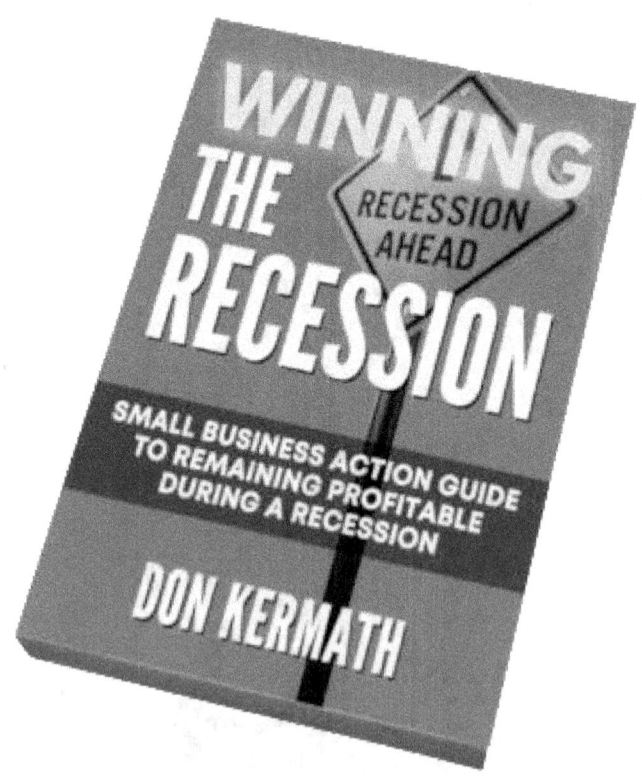

www.ingramcontent.com/pod-product-compliance
Lightning Source LLC
Chambersburg PA
CBHW070316220526
45465CB00004B/1873